THE BALD EAGLE

Author: Kelli L. Hicks

Rourke
Publishing LLC
Vero Beach, Florida 32964

www.rourkepublishing.com

PHOTO CREDITS: © FloridaStock: page 5, 8, 14, 15 18 ; © Maxim Bolotnikov: © Jeff Banke: page 7; © Bob Blanchard: page 9, 13; © PhotoDisc: page 10; © Stephen Inglis: page 11; © nialat: page 13; © Richard Langs: page 16; © Tony Campbel: page I7; © Matt Ragen: page 21; © Dave Menke-wiki: page 22; © Jill Lang: page 23; © U.S. AIR FORCE PHOTO BY JERRON BARNETT: page 25; © Eric Isselée: page 26; © Petty Officer 2nd Class Molly A. Burgess, USN: page 27; © Candy Hood: page 29; © Karla Caspari: page 30.

Editor: Jeanne Sturm

Cover design by: Nicola Stratford, bdpublishing.com
Interior design by: Heather Botto

Library of Congress Cataloging-in-Publication Data

Hicks, Kelli L.
  The bald eagle / Kelli L. Hicks.
    p. cm. -- (American symbols and landmarks)
  ISBN 978-1-60472-342-7 41037895   6/09
  1. Bald eagle--United States--Juvenile literature.
  CD5610 .H525 2009
  929.90973 22
                              2008014135

Printed in the USA

CG/CG

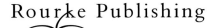

Rourke Publishing

www.rourkepublishing.com – rourke@rourkepublishing.com
Post Office Box 3328, Vero Beach, FL 32964

Table of Contents

A National Symbol

Have you ever looked up in the sky and seen a beautiful bird with a white head and neck? Have you watched its outspread wings as it gracefully coasts through the air? If the answer is yes, you may have seen a bald eagle.

The bald eagle is an important **symbol** for the United States of America. You will find the eagle on the back of a quarter, and on the great seal of the United States. The Continental Congress chose the bald eagle on June 20, 1782 as our national bird and it appears on the national emblem.

There are many reasons why it was chosen. The bald eagle has majestic looks and tends to live a very long life. Also, the bald eagle is the only eagle unique to North America.

There is a story that came from the Revolutionary War that also explains why some people wanted to choose the eagle as our symbol. A battle raged during the course of the Revolution that happened to be near a nest of sleeping eagles. The fighting woke the eagles and they began to fly with their wings spread grandly.

As the battle continued, the eagles circled above the heads of the fighting men. The birds were crying out and shrieking. The patriots believed they were yelling for freedom.

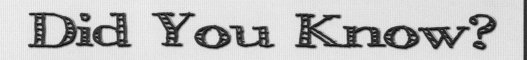

Did You Know?

Did you know that Benjamin Franklin wanted a turkey to be the national bird? He felt that eagles were birds of "bad moral character" who stole prey from other animals. He explained that the turkey was more respectable and silly, but courageous.

Benjamin Franklin

7

Where They Live

Bald eagles are found in Canada, northern Mexico, and many parts of the United States. Eagles prefer to nest near seacoasts, rivers, or lakes. About half the world's 70,000 bald eagles live in Alaska.

Scientists sort eagle types into four categories based on their appearance and behavior. They place the bald eagle in the group known as a sea or fish eagle. Bald eagles that live in the northern areas are **migratory** while bald eagles that live in Florida, Mexico, and other southern areas remain in the same location year round.

What They Look Like

A bald eagle's appearance is similar for both males and females. They both have yellow feet and beaks. The beaks are strong and can tear into meat easily. There are no feathers on the legs or feet. The eagle's feet have sharp **talons** that they use to pick up prey.

FUN FACT

Did you know that over 7,000 feathers cover an eagle's body?

You can easily recognize bald eagles by their white head and neck. Blackish brown colored feathers cover the rest of the body.

An eagle can see a fish in water or an animal on the ground from where it is flying in the sky. An eagle's vision is two to three times better than human eyesight.

An eagle can spot prey that is up to two miles away!

The eagle actually has three eyelids. One of the eyelids is clear and helps to protect the eagle's eyes and to keep the eyes clean.

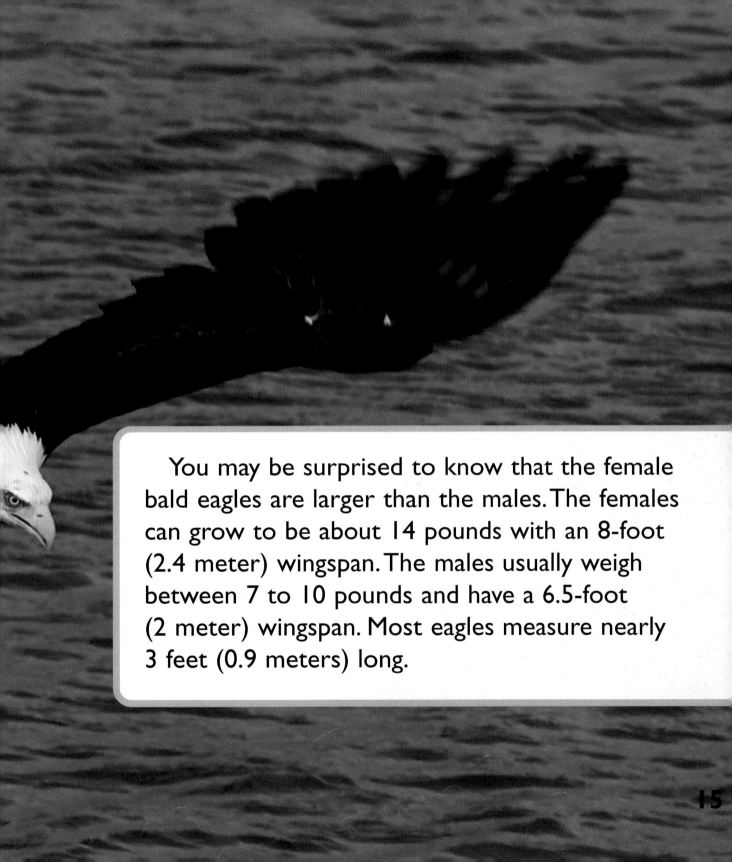

You may be surprised to know that the female bald eagles are larger than the males. The females can grow to be about 14 pounds with an 8-foot (2.4 meter) wingspan. The males usually weigh between 7 to 10 pounds and have a 6.5-foot (2 meter) wingspan. Most eagles measure nearly 3 feet (0.9 meters) long.

Nesting

Scientists discovered that bald eagles mate for life. An eagle will show off to try to find a mate. He may perform fancy dives or somersaults to attract attention. Once an eagle finds a mate, the two birds will stay together as a couple until one of the birds dies. Together they build a nest in the top of a large tree, usually near a lake, river, or other water source. Bald eagles will reuse the same nest year after year.

A typical nest reaches a diameter of 5 feet (1.5 meters), but eagles will continue to add on to their nests annually. Some nests may reach a size of 10 feet (3 meters) or larger, and weigh as much as 2,000 pounds. Bald eagles have long lives. They can live in the wild 30 years or more.

What They Eat

What do eagles eat?

Bald eagles are birds of prey. That means eagles rely on other animals as food. Bald eagles are mainly fish eaters, but will eat ducks or other small animals if that **prey** is the easiest to obtain. Eagles will fish in both fresh and salt water. Once an eagle spots its prey, it will swoop down and grab the animal out of the water with its strong talons.

A bald eagle can carry prey as heavy as 4 pounds. Sometimes, an eagle will feast on **carrion**, which is a dead and decaying animal. Eagles will sometimes steal food from other birds.

FUN FACT

Did you know that an eagle has no teeth? It rips food apart using its strong beak.

Eggs

Once an eagle reaches maturity at the age of four to five, it is able to reproduce. Eagles lay up to three eggs at one time. The egg must be incubated for a period of 35 days.

During **incubation** one parent remains in the nest not only to keep the eggs warm, but also to protect the eggs from other animals that might want to eat them.

Both the male and the female take turns caring for the eggs, but the female generally spends the most time in the nest. It is interesting to note that the male will bring sprigs of **conifer** branches to the nest. Some scientists believe they bring the sprigs to deodorize the nest or that they might use them to provide shade. Unfortunately, no one knows for sure. Bald eagles prefer a peaceful and quiet environment in which to breed.

Eaglets

When the eggs hatch, the chicks are small and grayish-white. Their feathers are soft and downy. They have weak legs and limited vision. It is up to the parents to protect them from danger.

Eagles feed their young by tearing small pieces of meat from their prey with their beaks. They place the meat in the mouth of the chicks and encourage them to eat.

FUN FACTS

The eaglet uses an egg tooth to hatch out of the egg. The tooth breaks off after about a month. The parents will always feed the eaglet that hatched first before they feed the others. Why do you think they do that?

By the time the chicks are 6 weeks old, they are nearly the size of their parents! This is also the time when they shed the downy feathers, and the blackish brown adult feathers begin to grow. Baby eagles, called **eaglets**, will try to fly for the first time when they are 10 to 13 weeks old.

23

Decline in Numbers

When the first settlers arrived in America, the number of bald eagles was probably close to a half million. As more settlers arrived, they shared the same fishing areas as the eagles. People built homes and cut down trees that may have housed an eagle's nest. Later, people developed weapons which they used to hunt eagles. Some farmers shot eagles because they thought the eagles were eating their chickens.

By the 1930s, people recognized that the numbers were steadily decreasing. By 1940, the government passed the Bald Eagle Act, which had penalties for humans caught hunting or bothering the birds.

Another problem that caused a decline in the number of eagles was that people began spraying the **pesticide** DDT. This pesticide covered the plants that small animals ate.

Once the eagles ate the contaminated animals, the adults and the eggs became damaged. The eggs' shells became too thin to protect the chick inside and they never hatched. In 1976, researchers officially added the bald eagle to the National Endangered Species list.

Protection

Eventually, people realized how serious the situation had become. The government finally banned the use of DDT and, over time, the eagle was one of the few species on the endangered list that was able to recover its numbers and remove the threat of extinction.

On June 28, 2007, the bald eagle was removed from the endangered species list. The Migratory Bird Treaty Act continues to protect the bald eagle in the wild. The Bald and Golden Eagle Protection Act also helps to protect the eagle population by providing harsh penalties for people caught harming or hunting eagles.

Captivity

Some humans also helped to improve the numbers in the eagle population by raising and breeding eagles in captivity. Scientists removed bald eagle eggs from the nest and incubated them in an artificial environment. Once

hatched, scientists returned the chicks to the nest of foster parents who were able to care for the eaglets.

Scientists used a program called **hacking** to increase the eagle population. Eight week old eaglets were placed in a man-made nest in an area where the eagle population was diminished.

Scientists fed the eaglets and watched them as they lived in an enclosed environment. When they could fly, they opened the enclosure and the eaglets integrated into the wild.

Myths and Legends

There are many Native American myths and stories about the bald eagle. The Comanche tribe tells a story about a chief who lost his young son. The son was turned into the first eagle to answer the father's prayers for his return. The Comanche Eagle Dance commemorates this legend. The Pawnee also honor the eagle with songs, poems, and dances.

The Plains Indian tribes celebrate with the Sun Dance. During the dance, a medicine man will wave a fan made from eagle feathers and point to people who need medical care or healing. He then points the fan to the sky so that the eagle may carry the prayers to the heavens.

Glossary

carrion (KAIR-ee-uhn): dead and decaying flesh

conifer (KON-uh-fur): an evergreen tree that produces cones

eaglet (EE-glit): a baby eagle

hacking (HAK-ing): a process used by scientists to increase the eagle population

incubation (ING-kyuh-bay-shun): the period of time necessary to keep an egg warm until it hatches

migratory (MYE-gruh-tor-ee): characterized by movement from one country or region to another

pesticide (PESS-tuh-side): a chemical used to kill pests such as insects

prey (PRAY): an animal that is hunted by another animal for food

symbol (SIM-buhl): a design or an object that represents something else

talons (TAL-uhns): the sharp claws of a bird of prey

Further Reading

Goldish, Meish. *Bald Eagles: A Chemical Nightmare.* Bearport Publishing, Inc, 2007.

Hempstead, Anne. *Land of the Free: The Bald Eagle.* Heinemann, 2006.

Wilcox, Charlotte. *Bald Eagles.* Carolrhoda Books, Inc, 2003.

Websites

www.baldeagleinfo.com

www.birds.cornell.edu/allaboutbirds/birdguide/bald_eagle.html

www.bensguide.gpo.gov/3-5/symbols/eagle.html

Index

About the Author

Kelli Hicks is an educational consultant with over fourteen years of teaching and administrative experience. As a charter member of the Tampa Bay Area Writing Project, Kelli works to share her love of reading and writing with both teachers and students. She currently lives in Tampa, Florida.